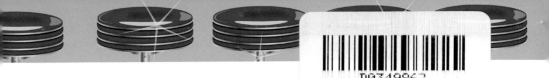

CONTENTS

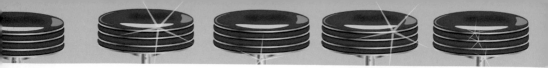

STRAWBERRY RHUBARB PIE

MAKES 8 SERVINGS

Double-Crust Pie Pastry
(recipe follows)

1½ cups sugar

½ cup cornstarch

2 tablespoons quick-cooking
tapioca

1 tablespoon grated lemon
peel

¼ teaspoon ground allspice

4 cups sliced rhubarb
(1-inch pieces)

3 cups sliced fresh
strawberries

1 egg, lightly beaten

1 Prepare Double-Crust Pie Pastry. Preheat oven to 425°F.

2 Roll out one pastry disc into 11-inch circle on floured surface. Line
9-inch pie plate with pastry.

3 Combine sugar, cornstarch, tapioca, lemon peel and allspice in large
bowl. Add rhubarb and strawberries; toss to coat. Pour into crust.

4 Roll out remaining pastry disc into 10-inch circle; cut into ½-inch-wide
strips. Arrange in lattice design over fruit. Seal and flute edge. Brush
pastry with beaten egg.

5 Bake 50 minutes or until filling is thick and bubbly and crust is
golden brown. Cool on wire rack. Serve warm or at room temperature.

DOUBLE-CRUST PIE PASTRY

Combine 2½ cups all-purpose flour, 1 teaspoon salt and 1 teaspoon
sugar in large bowl. Cut in 1 cup (2 sticks) cubed butter with pastry
blender or two knives until mixture resembles coarse crumbs.
Drizzle ⅓ cup water over flour mixture, 2 tablespoons at a time,
stirring just until dough comes together. Divide dough in half. Shape
each half into disc; wrap in plastic wrap. Refrigerate 30 minutes.
(Dough may be refrigerated up to 2 days or frozen up to 1 month
before using. If frozen, thaw in refrigerator before using.)

NECTARINE-RASPBERRY COBBLER

MAKES 6 SERVINGS

3 cups sliced peeled nectarines or peaches (about 1¼ pounds)

½ cup fresh raspberries

3 tablespoons sugar, divided

1 tablespoon cornstarch

½ teaspoon ground cinnamon

¾ cup all-purpose flour

1 teaspoon grated lemon peel

¾ teaspoon baking powder

¼ teaspoon salt

⅛ teaspoon baking soda

3 tablespoons cold butter, cut into small pieces

½ cup buttermilk

1 Preheat oven to 375°F. Combine nectarines and raspberries in large bowl. Combine 2 tablespoons sugar, cornstarch and cinnamon in small bowl. Add to fruit; toss to coat. Pour into 8-inch round baking dish.

2 Combine flour, lemon peel, baking powder, salt, baking soda and remaining 1 tablespoon sugar in medium bowl. Cut in butter with pastry blender or two knives until mixture resembles coarse crumbs. Stir in buttermilk until blended. Drop dough in 6 equal spoonfuls over fruit.

3 Bake 25 to 27 minutes or until filling is bubbly and topping is just beginning to brown. Serve warm.

TIP

One pound frozen unsweetened peach slices and ½ cup frozen unsweetened raspberries may be substituted for the fresh fruit. Let the peach slices stand at room temperature until almost thawed, at least 2 hours. Use the raspberries frozen. Bake an additional 3 to 5 minutes or until the filling is bubbly and the topping is beginning to brown.

CRANBERRY APPLE CRISP

MAKES 8 SERVINGS | PREP TIME: 25 minutes **BAKE TIME:** 50 minutes

FILLING

- ½ cup granulated sugar
- 3 tablespoons ARGO® or KINGSFORD'S® Corn Starch
- 1 teaspoon SPICE ISLANDS® Ground Saigon Cinnamon
- ½ teaspoon SPICE ISLANDS® Ground Nutmeg
- 5 to 6 cups peeled, cubed tart apples
- 1 cup fresh or frozen cranberries
- ½ cup KARO® Light Corn Syrup
- 1 teaspoon grated orange peel

TOPPING

- ½ cup walnuts or quick oats (not instant)
- ⅓ cup packed brown sugar
- ¼ cup all-purpose flour
- ¼ (½ stick) butter or margarine

1 Mix granulated sugar, corn starch, cinnamon and nutmeg in a large bowl. Add apples, cranberries, corn syrup and orange peel; toss to combine. Spoon into shallow 2-quart baking dish.

2 Combine walnuts, brown sugar and flour in a small bowl. With a pastry blender or 2 knives, cut in butter until crumbly.

3 Top apple filling with walnut mixture.

4 Bake at 350°F for 50 minutes or until cranberries and apples are tender and juices that bubble up in center are shiny and clear. Cool slightly; serve warm.

CREAMY MILK CHOCOLATE PUDDING PIE

MAKES 6 TO 8 SERVINGS

⅔ cup sugar

6 tablespoons cornstarch

2 tablespoons HERSHEY'S Cocoa

½ teaspoon salt

3 cups milk

4 egg yolks

2 tablespoons butter or margarine, softened

1 tablespoon vanilla extract

5 HERSHEY'S Milk Chocolate bars (1.55 ounces each), broken into pieces

1 packaged chocolate crumb crust (6 ounces)

Sweetened whipped cream or whipped topping

Additional HERSHEY'S Milk Chocolate Bar (1.55 ounces), cut into sections along score lines (optional)

1 Stir together sugar, cornstarch, cocoa and salt in 2-quart saucepan. Combine milk and egg yolks in bowl or container with pouring spout. Gradually blend milk mixture into sugar mixture.

2 Cook over medium heat, stirring constantly, until mixture comes to a boil. Boil and stir 1 minute. Remove from heat; stir in butter and vanilla. Add chocolate bar pieces; stir until bars are melted and mixture is well blended. Pour into crumb crust; press plastic wrap onto filling. Cool. Refrigerate several hours or until chilled and firm. Remove plastic wrap. Garnish with whipped cream and chocolate bar sections. Cover; refrigerate leftovers.

PLUM RHUBARB CRUMBLE

MAKES 6 TO 8 SERVINGS

1½ pounds plums, each pitted and cut into 8 wedges (4 cups)

1½ pounds rhubarb, cut into ½-inch pieces (5 cups)

1 cup granulated sugar

1 teaspoon finely grated fresh ginger

¼ teaspoon ground nutmeg

3 tablespoons cornstarch

¾ cup old-fashioned oats

½ cup all-purpose flour

½ cup packed brown sugar

½ cup sliced almonds, toasted*

¼ teaspoon salt

½ cup (1 stick) cold butter, cut into small pieces

To toast almonds, spread on ungreased baking sheet. Bake in preheated 350°F oven 5 minutes or until golden brown, stirring frequently.

1 Combine plums, rhubarb, granulated sugar, ginger and nutmeg in large bowl; toss to coat. Cover and let stand at room temperature 2 hours.

2 Preheat oven to 375°F. Spray 9-inch round or square baking dish with nonstick cooking spray. Line baking sheet with foil.

3 Pour juices from fruit into small saucepan; bring to a boil over medium-high heat. Cook about 12 minutes or until reduced to syrupy consistency, stirring occasionally. Stir in cornstarch until well blended. Stir mixture into bowl with fruit; pour into prepared baking dish.

4 Combine oats, flour, brown sugar, almonds and salt in medium bowl; mix well. Add butter; mix with fingertips until butter is evenly distributed and mixture is clumpy. Sprinkle evenly over fruit mixture. Place baking dish on prepared baking sheet.

5 Bake about 50 minutes or until filling is bubbly and topping is golden brown. Cool on wire rack 1 hour before serving.

BROWN BUTTER BLUEBERRY PEACH COBBLER

MAKES 8 SERVINGS

3 tablespoons butter

4 packages (16 ounces each) frozen sliced peaches, thawed and drained

1 cup fresh blueberries

½ cup packed brown sugar

¼ cup all-purpose flour

½ teaspoon vanilla

¼ teaspoon ground nutmeg

1¼ cups biscuit baking mix

⅓ cup milk

2 tablespoons butter, melted

2 tablespoons granulated sugar

1 Preheat oven to 375°F.

2 Melt 3 tablespoons butter in large skillet (not nonstick) over medium heat. Cook and stir about 3 minutes or until butter has nutty aroma and turns light brown in color. Add peaches; cook and stir 2 minutes.

3 Combine peaches, blueberries, brown sugar, flour, vanilla and nutmeg in large bowl; toss to coat. Pour into 2-quart oval baking dish. Bake 10 minutes.

4 Meanwhile, combine baking mix, milk, 2 tablespoons melted butter and granulated sugar in medium bowl; mix well. Drop 8 equal spoonfuls of batter over warm fruit mixture.

5 Bake 30 to 35 minutes or until biscuits are deep golden brown and cooked on bottom. Cool on wire rack 10 minutes. Serve warm.

CLASSIC APPLE PIE

MAKES 8 SERVINGS

1 package (15 ounces) refrigerated pie crusts (2 crusts)

6 cups sliced peeled Granny Smith, Crispin or other firm-fleshed apples (about 6 medium)

½ cup sugar

1 tablespoon cornstarch

2 teaspoons lemon juice

½ teaspoon vanilla

½ teaspoon ground cinnamon

⅛ teaspoon salt

⅛ teaspoon ground nutmeg

⅛ teaspoon ground cloves

1 tablespoon whipping cream

1 Let one crust stand at room temperature 15 minutes. Preheat oven to 350°F. Line 9-inch pie plate with crust.

2 Combine apples, sugar, cornstarch, lemon juice, vanilla, cinnamon, salt, nutmeg and cloves in large bowl; toss to coat. Pour into crust. Place second crust over apples; crimp edge to seal. Cut four slits in top crust; brush with cream.

3 Bake 40 minutes or until crust is golden brown. Cool completely on wire rack.

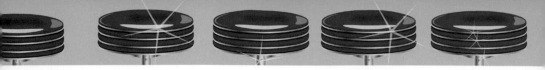

FRESH BERRY-BERRY COBBLER

MAKES 6 SERVINGS | **PREP TIME:** 10 minutes **START TO FINISH TIME:** 35 minutes

¼ cup sugar

1 teaspoon cornstarch

12 ounces fresh raspberries

8 ounces fresh blueberries

¼ cup CREAM OF WHEAT® Hot Cereal (Instant, 1-minute, 2½-minute or 10-minute cook time), uncooked

¼ cup all-purpose flour

¼ cup ground almonds

2 teaspoons baking powder

¼ teaspoon salt

¼ cup (½ stick) butter, cut into small pieces, softened

¼ cup milk

1 egg

1 tablespoon sugar

Ice cream or whipped cream (optional)

1 Preheat oven to 450°F. Blend sugar and cornstarch in mixing bowl. Add berries and toss to coat. Pour into 8-inch square baking pan; set aside.

2 Combine Cream of Wheat, flour, almonds, baking powder and salt in food processor. Add butter; pulse several times until well combined. Add milk and egg; pulse until mixed thoroughly. Spread evenly over fruit mixture. Sprinkle sugar over top.

3 Bake 20 minutes. Let stand 5 minutes before serving. Serve in shallow bowls with ice cream or whipped cream, if desired.

TIP

For an elegant presentation, serve in a martini glass and top with a fresh sprig of mint.

DOLE® VERY PEACHY PIE

MAKES 1 (9-INCH) PIE | PREP TIME: 20 minutes **BAKE TIME:** 45 minutes

¾ cup sugar

3½ tablespoons minute tapioca

¼ teaspoon salt

6 cups DOLE® Frozen Sliced Peaches, thawed

1 tablespoon lemon juice

¼ teaspoon grated lemon peel

Pastry for 9-inch double-crust pie

2 tablespoons butter **or** margarine, cut into small pieces

Milk

- **Combine** sugar, tapioca and salt in small bowl.
- **Combine** peaches, lemon juice, lemon peel and sugar mixture in large bowl; mix well.
- **Roll** out half of pastry and fit into pie pan. Roll out remaining pastry.
- **Spoon** peach mixture into pie pan. Dot with butter. Top with remaining pastry; trim, turn under and flute edges.
- **Cut** a few slits in top. Brush lightly with milk and sprinkle with additional sugar, if desired.
- **Lightly** cover edges with thin strips of aluminum foil. Bake at 425°F 20 minutes. Remove foil and bake 20 to 25 minutes longer or until golden brown. Cool on wire rack.

FARMHOUSE LEMON MERINGUE PIE

MAKES 8 SERVINGS

1 (9-inch) frozen pie crust

4 eggs, at room temperature

3 tablespoons lemon juice

2 tablespoons butter, melted

2 teaspoons grated lemon peel

3 drops yellow food coloring (optional)

⅔ cup sugar, divided

1 cup cold water

¼ cup cornstarch

⅛ teaspoon salt

¼ teaspoon vanilla

1 Preheat oven to 425°F. Bake pie crust according to package directions.

2 Separate eggs; discard 2 egg yolks. Combine lemon juice, butter, lemon peel and food coloring, if desired, in small bowl.

3 Reserve 2 tablespoons sugar. Combine water, remaining sugar, cornstarch and salt in medium saucepan; whisk until smooth. Bring to a boil over medium-high heat, whisking constantly. Reduce heat to medium; boil 1 minute, whisking constantly. Remove from heat.

4 Stir ¼ cup hot sugar mixture into egg yolks in medium bowl, whisking constantly. Slowly whisk egg yolk mixture back into hot sugar mixture. Cook over medium heat 3 minutes, whisking constantly. Remove from heat; stir in lemon juice mixture until well blended. Pour into baked pie crust.

5 Beat egg whites in large bowl with electric mixer at high speed until soft peaks form. Slowly beat in reserved 2 tablespoons sugar and vanilla; beat until stiff peaks form. Spread meringue over pie filling, making sure meringue completely covers filling and touches edge of pie crust.

6 Bake 5 to 10 minutes or until meringue is lightly browned. Cool completely on wire rack. Cover with plastic wrap; refrigerate 8 hours or overnight until filling is firm and pie is thoroughly chilled.

DOUBLE PLUM COBBLER

MAKES 8 SERVINGS

FILLING

10 red or black plums (about 2½ pounds), pitted and cut into ½-inch wedges

⅔ cup plum preserves

⅓ cup sugar

2 tablespoons cornstarch

¼ teaspoon almond extract

BISCUITS

1 cup all-purpose flour

2 tablespoons plus 2 teaspoons sugar, divided

1 teaspoon baking powder

¼ teaspoon baking soda

½ teaspoon salt

5 tablespoons cold butter, cut into small pieces

½ cup plus 2 tablespoons buttermilk, divided

1 Preheat oven to 375°F. Spray 2-quart oval baking dish with nonstick cooking spray.

2 Combine plums, preserves, ⅓ cup sugar, cornstarch and almond extract in medium bowl; toss to coat. Spoon into prepared baking dish. Bake 20 minutes.

3 Meanwhile, combine flour, 2 tablespoons sugar, baking powder, baking soda and salt in medium bowl; mix well. Cut in butter with pastry blender or two knives until mixture resembles coarse crumbs. Add ½ cup buttermilk; stir just until moistened. Knead dough one or two times in bowl until it holds together. Shape dough into a disc. Wrap with plastic wrap; refrigerate 15 minutes.

4 Roll out dough to scant ½-inch thickness on floured surface. Cut out about 15 biscuits with 2-inch biscuit cutter, pressing dough scraps together and rerolling if necessary. Arrange biscuits over warm plum mixture. Brush tops of biscuits with remaining 2 tablespoons buttermilk; sprinkle with remaining 2 teaspoons sugar.

5 Bake in center of oven about 30 minutes or until biscuits are lightly browned. Cover loosely with foil; bake 10 minutes or until filling is thick and bubbly. Cool on wire rack 30 minutes before serving.

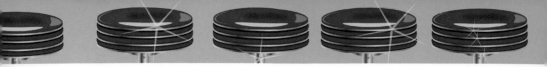

SWEET POTATO PECAN PIE

MAKES 8 SERVINGS

1 unbaked 9-inch deep-dish pie crust

1½ cups pecan halves

½ cup light corn syrup

1 egg white

2 cups puréed cooked sweet potatoes (about 1½ pounds uncooked sweet potatoes)

⅓ cup packed brown sugar

1 teaspoon vanilla

½ teaspoon ground cinnamon

¼ teaspoon salt

Pinch *each* ground nutmeg and ground cloves

2 eggs, beaten

Whipped cream (optional)

1 Preheat oven to 400°F. Prick holes in bottom of crust with fork. Bake 10 minutes or until lightly browned. Cool completely on wire rack.

2 *Reduce oven temperature to 350°F.* Combine pecans, corn syrup and egg white in small bowl. Combine sweet potatoes, brown sugar, vanilla, cinnamon, salt, nutmeg and cloves in large bowl. Stir in eggs until blended. Spread sweet potato mixture evenly in crust; top with pecan mixture.

3 Bake 45 minutes or until filling is puffed and topping is golden brown. Cool completely on wire rack. Top with whipped cream, if desired.

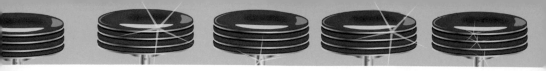

CRISPY CHOCOLATE ICE CREAM MUD PIE

MAKES 8 SERVINGS

½ cup HERSHEY'S Syrup

⅓ cup HERSHEY'S SPECIAL DARK Chocolate Chips or HERSHEY'S Semi-Sweet Chocolate Chips

2 cups crisp rice cereal

4 cups (1 quart) vanilla ice cream, divided

4 cups (1 quart) chocolate ice cream, divided

Additional HERSHEY'S Syrup

1 Butter 9-inch pie plate.

2 Place ½ cup chocolate syrup and chocolate chips in medium microwave-safe bowl. Microwave at MEDIUM (50%) 45 seconds or until hot; stir until smooth. Reserve ¼ cup chocolate syrup mixture; set aside. Add cereal to remaining chocolate syrup mixture, stirring until well coated; cool slightly.

3 Press cereal mixture, using back of spoon, evenly on bottom and up side of prepared pie plate to form crust. Place in freezer 15 to 20 minutes or until crust is firm. Spread half of vanilla ice cream in crust; spoon reserved ¼ cup chocolate syrup mixture over layer. Spread half of chocolate ice cream over sauce.

4 Top with alternating scoops of vanilla and chocolate ice cream. Cover; return to freezer until serving time. Drizzle with additional chocolate syrup just before serving.

EASY COCONUT BANANA CREAM PIE

MAKES 8 SERVINGS

1 *prebaked* 9-inch (4-cup volume) deep-dish pie shell

1 can (14 ounces) NESTLÉ® CARNATION® Sweetened Condensed Milk

1 cup cold water

1 package (3.4 ounces) vanilla or banana cream instant pudding and pie filling mix

1 cup flaked coconut

1 container (8 ounces) frozen whipped topping, thawed, *divided*

2 medium bananas, sliced, dipped in lemon juice

Toasted or tinted flaked coconut (optional)

COMBINE sweetened condensed milk and water in large bowl. Add pudding mix and coconut; mix well. Fold in *1½ cups* whipped topping.

ARRANGE single layer of bananas on bottom of pie crust. Pour filling into crust. Top with *remaining* whipped topping. Refrigerate for 4 hours or until well set. Top with toasted or tinted coconut.

NOTE

To make 2 pies, divide filling between 2 *prebaked* 9-inch (2-cup volume *each*) pie crusts. Top with *remaining* whipped topping.

ACKNOWLEDGMENTS

The publisher would like to thank the companies listed below for the use of their recipes and photographs in this publication.

ACH Food Companies, Inc.

Cream of Wheat® Cereal, A Division of B&G Foods North America, Inc.

Dole Food Company, Inc.

The Hershey Company

Nestlé USA